Maths Tests Ages 8–9

National Tests

KS2 Year 4

Two full test papers with detailed answers and advice

◪SCHOLASTIC

Scholastic Distribution Centre, Bosworth Avenue,
Tournament Fields, Warwick, CV34 6UQ

Scholastic Ireland, 89E Lagan Road, Dublin Industrial Estate,
Glasnevin, Dublin, D11 HP5F

www.scholastic.co.uk

© 2018 Scholastic

23456789   3456789012

A CIP catalogue record for this book is available from the
British Library.

ISBN 978-1407-18300-8

Printed by Replika Press, India.

The book is made of materials from well-managed,
FSC®-certified forests and other controlled sources.

Author and series editor
Paul Hollin

Editorial team
Rachel Morgan, Jenny Wilcox, Mark Walker,
Mary Nathan, Janette Ratcliffe and
Christine Vaughan

Illustrations
Tom Heard and Moreno Chiacchiera

Design
Nicolle Thomas, Alice Duggan
and Oxford Designers and Illustrators

Cover illustrations
Istock/calvindexter and Tomek.gr / Shutterstock/Visual Generation

Acknowledgements

Extracts from Department for Education website ©
Crown Copyright. Reproduced under the terms of the
Open Government Licence (OGL). www.nationalarchives.
gov.uk/doc/open-government-licence/version/3/

Every effort has been made to trace copyright holders
for the works reproduced in this publication, and the
publishers apologise or any inadvertent omissions.

Contents
Mathematics: Year 4

Contents	Page
Introduction	
About this book	4
About the tests	5
Advice for parents and carers	6
Advice for children	7
Test coverage	8
Tests	
Test A	10
Test B	71
Marks & guidance	
Marking and assessing the papers	132
Formal written methods	134
National standard in maths	135
Mark scheme: Test A	136
• Paper 1	136
• Paper 2	138
• Paper 3	141
Mark scheme: Test B	144
• Paper 1	144
• Paper 2	146
• Paper 3	148

About this book

This book provides you with practice papers to help support children with end-of-year tests and to assess which skills need further development.

Using the practice papers

The practice papers in this book can be used as you would any other practice materials. The children need to be familiar with specific test-focused skills, such as ensuring equipment functions properly, leaving questions if they seem too difficult, working at a suitable pace for the tests and checking through their work.

If you choose to use the papers for revising content rather than practising tests do be aware of the time factor. These tests are short at only 30 or 40 minutes per paper, as they are testing the degree of competence children have.

Equipment

The following equipment will be needed for all test papers.

- pencil/black pen
- eraser

For papers 2 and 3 you may need:

- ruler (mm and cm)
- angle measurer / protractor

About the tests

Each maths test has three papers:

- Paper 1: arithmetic – these are context-free calculations. The children have 30 minutes to answer the questions. 40 marks are available.
- Paper 2 and Paper 3: reasoning – these are mathematical reasoning problems both in context and out of context. The children have 40 minutes per paper to answer the questions. 35 marks are available per paper.

The papers should be taken in order and children may have a break between papers. All of the tests broadly increase in difficulty as they progress, and it is not expected that all children will be able to answer all of the questions.

The marks available for each question are shown in the test paper next to each question and are also shown next to each answer in the mark scheme.

Advice for parents and carers

How this book will help

This book will support your child to get ready for the school-based end-of-year tests in maths. It provides valuable practice and help on the responses and content expected of Year 4 children aged 8–9 years.

In the weeks leading up to the school tests, your child may be given plenty of practice, revision and tips to give them the best possible chance to demonstrate their knowledge and understanding. It is helpful to try to practise outside of school and many children benefit from extra input. This book will help your child to prepare and build their confidence.

In this book you will find two mathematics tests. The layout and format of each test closely matches those used in the National Tests so your child will become familiar with what to expect and get used to the style of the tests. There is a comprehensive answer section and guidance about how to mark the questions.

Tips

- Make sure that you allow your child to take the test in a quiet environment where they are not likely to be interrupted or distracted.

- Make sure your child has a flat surface to work on, with plenty of space to spread out and good light.

- Emphasise the importance of reading and re-reading a question.

- These tests are similar to the ones your child will take in May in Year 6 and they therefore give you a good idea of strengths and areas for development. When you have found areas that require some more practice, it is useful to go over these again and practise similar types of question with your child.

- Go through the tests again together, identify any gaps in learning and address any misconceptions or areas of misunderstanding. If you are unsure of anything yourself, then make an appointment to see your child's teacher who will be able to help and advise further.

- Practising little and often will enable your child to build up confidence and skills over a period of time.

Advice for children

- Revise and practise regularly.
- Spend some time each week practising.
- Focus on the areas you are least confident in to get better.
- Get a good night's sleep and eat a healthy breakfast.
- Be on time for school.
- Make sure you have all the things you need.
- Avoid stressful situations before a test.
- If a questions asks you to 'Show your method' then there will be marks if you get the method correct even if your answer is wrong.
- Leave out questions you do not understand and come back to them when you have completed those you can do.
- Check that you haven't missed any questions or pages out.
- Try to spend the last five minutes checking your work. Do your answers look about right?
- If you have time to spare and have a few questions unanswered, just have a go – you don't lose marks for trying.

Test coverage

The test content is divided into strands and sub-strands. These are listed, for each question, in a table at the end of every test to allow tracking of difficulties. In a small number of cases, where practical equipment such as containers would be required, these aspects are not tested.

Strand	Sub-strand
Number and place value	counting (in multiples)
	read, write, order and compare numbers
	place value; Roman numerals
	identify, represent and estimate; rounding
	negative numbers
	number problems
Addition, subtraction, multiplication and division (calculations)	add/subtract mentally
	add/subtract using written methods
	estimates, use inverses and check
	add/subtract to solve problems
	multiply/divide mentally
	multiply/divide using written methods
	solve problems (commutative, associative, distributive and all four operations)
Fractions	recognise, find, write, name and count fractions
	equivalent fractions
	compare and order fractions
	add/subtract fractions
	fractions/decimals equivalence
	rounding decimals
	compare and order decimals
	multiply/divide decimals
	solve problems with fractions and decimals
Measurement	compare, describe and order measures
	estimate, measure and read scales
	money
	telling time, ordering time, duration and units of time
	convert between metric units
	perimeter, area
	solve problems (money; length; mass/weight; capacity/volume)

■SCHOLASTIC National Curriculum SATs Tests

Strand	Sub-strand
Geometry – properties of shape	recognise and name common shapes
	describe properties and classify shapes
	draw and make shapes and relate 2D and 3D shapes (including nets)
	angles – measuring and properties
Geometry – position and direction	patterns
	describe position, direction and movement
	coordinates
Statistics	interpret and represent data
	solve problems involving data

Instructions Test A: Paper 1

You **may not** use a calculator to answer any questions in this test.

Questions and answers

- You have **30 minutes** to complete this test.
- Work as quickly and carefully as you can.
- Put your answer in the box for each question.

- If you cannot do one of the questions, **go on to the next one**. You can come back to it later if you have time.
- If you finish before the end, **go back and check your work**.

Marks

- The number next to each box at the side of the page tells you the maximum number of marks for each question.
- In this test, short division and long multiplication questions are worth **2 marks** each. You will be awarded 2 marks for a correct answer.
- You may get 1 mark for showing a formal method.

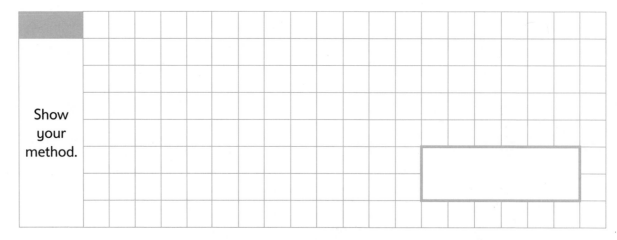

Show your method.

- All other questions are worth **1 mark** each.

Marks

1. $\frac{1}{2}$ of 6 =

1

2. 5 × 3 =

1

3. 19 + 9 =

1

4. $24 \div 6 =$

Marks

1

5. $4635 - 500 =$

1

6. $8 + 5 + 8 =$

1

Marks

7. $865 - 65 =$

1

8. $\dfrac{5}{7} - \dfrac{3}{7} =$

1

9. $20 + 35 =$

1

Test A: Paper 1

Marks

10. 7 × 5 =

1

11. 265 − 52 =

1

12. 3000 + 300 =

1

SCHOLASTIC National Curriculum SATs Tests

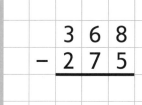
13.

Marks

$$\begin{array}{r} 3\ 6\ 8 \\ -\ 2\ 7\ 5 \\ \hline \end{array}$$

1

14. 0.1 + 0.1 =

1

15. $\frac{1}{6} + \frac{4}{6} =$

1

16. 10 × 20 =

Marks

1

17. 45 ÷ 5 =

1

18. 54 ÷ 10 =

1

19. 9375 − 6000 =

Marks

1

20. 12 × 120 =

1

21. 275 + 98 =

1

22. $63 \times 100 =$

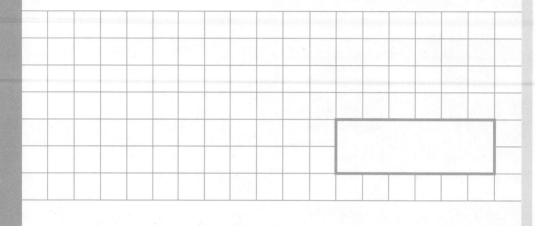

1

23. $1 - \frac{3}{8} =$

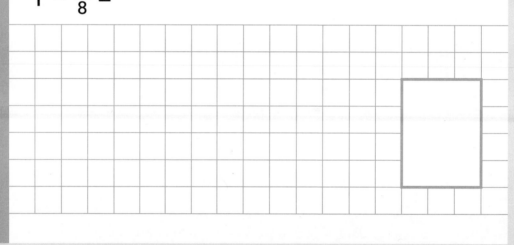

1

24. $23 + 31 + 45 =$

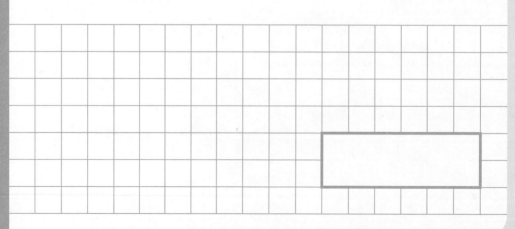

1

SCHOLASTIC National Curriculum SATs Tests

25.   600 ÷ 3 =

Marks

1

26.

```
    4  3  6
  ×       6
  _____
```

Show your method.

2

27. $3 \div 100 =$

Marks

1

28.

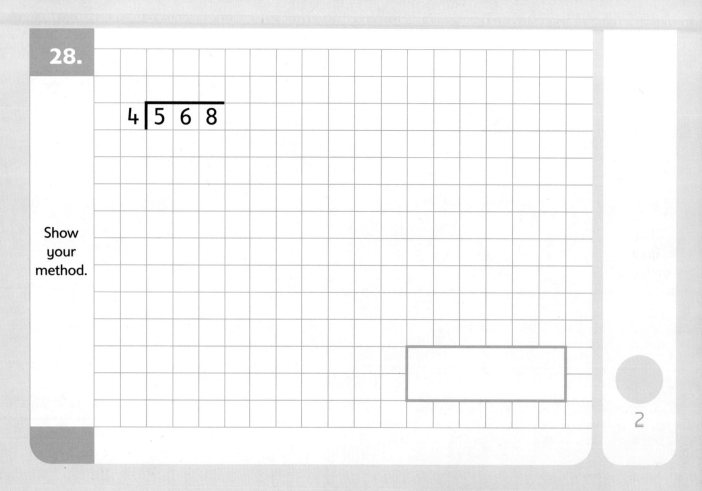

$4 \overline{)5\ 6\ 8}$

Show your method.

2

SCHOLASTIC National Curriculum SATs Tests

29. $2 \times 6 \times 5 =$

Marks

1

30.

```
   7 8 3 7
 − 5 1 4 6
 _____
```

1

31. $5384 − 998 =$

1

32.

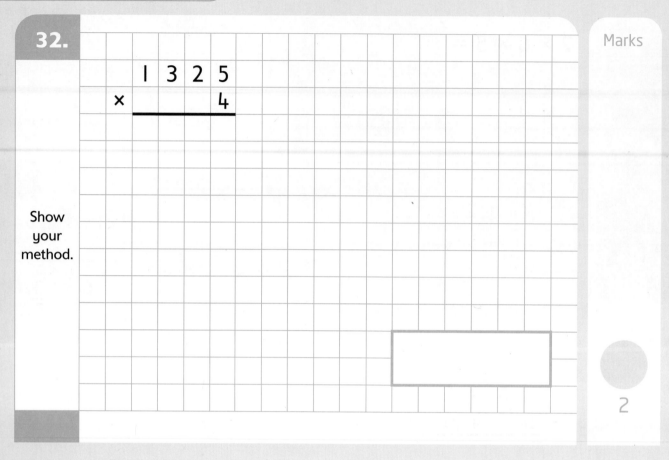

```
    1 3 2 5
  ×       4
```

Show your method.

2

33.

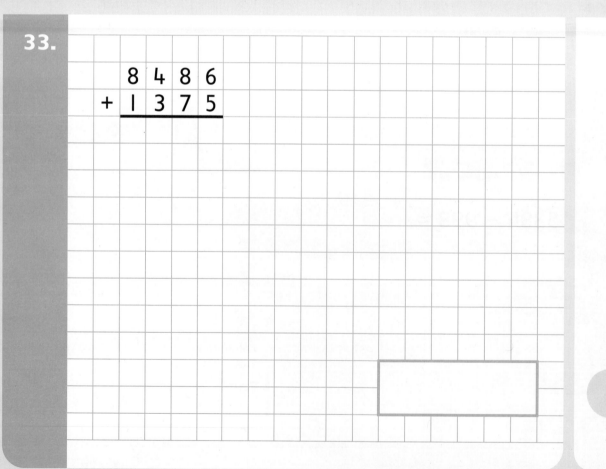

```
    8 4 8 6
  + 1 3 7 5
```

1

Marks

34. $\frac{3}{4}$ of 24 =

1

35. 5782 – 1111 =

1

36.

3 | 8 2 0

Show your method.

2

Test A: Paper 1 Marks

Q	Question	Possible marks	Actual marks	Q	Question	Possible marks	Actual marks
1	$\frac{1}{2}$ of 6	1		19	9375 − 6000	1	
2	5 × 3	1		20	12 × 120	1	
3	19 + 9	1		21	275 + 98	1	
4	24 ÷ 6	1		22	63 × 100	1	
5	4635 − 500	1		23	$1 - \frac{3}{8}$	1	
6	8 + 5 + 8	1		24	23 + 31 + 45	1	
7	865 − 65	1		25	600 ÷ 3	1	
8	$\frac{5}{7} - \frac{3}{7}$	1		26	$\begin{array}{r} 4\,3\,6 \\ \times\quad 6 \\ \hline \end{array}$	2	
9	20 + 35	1		27	3 ÷ 100	1	
10	7 × 5	1		28	$4\overline{)5\,6\,8}$	2	
11	265 − 52	1		29	2 × 6 × 5	1	
12	3000 + 300	1		30	$\begin{array}{r} 7\,8\,3\,7 \\ -\,5\,1\,4\,6 \\ \hline \end{array}$	1	
13	368 − 275	1		31	5384 − 998	1	
14	0.1 + 0.1	1		32	$\begin{array}{r} 1\,3\,2\,5 \\ \times\quad\ 4 \\ \hline \end{array}$	2	
15	$\frac{1}{6} + \frac{4}{6}$	1		33	$\begin{array}{r} 8\,4\,8\,6 \\ +\,1\,3\,7\,5 \\ \hline \end{array}$	1	
16	10 × 20	1		34	$\frac{3}{4}$ of 24	1	
17	45 ÷ 5	1		35	5782 − 1111	1	
18	54 ÷ 10	1		36	$3\overline{)8\,2\,0}$	2	
					Total	**40**	

- You have **40 minutes** for this test paper.
- You may **not use** a calculator to answer any questions in this test paper.
- Work as quickly and carefully as you can.
- Try to answer all the questions. If you cannot do one of the questions, **go on to the next one**. You can come back to it later, if you have time.
- If you finish before the end, **go back and check your work**.
- Ask your teacher if you are not sure what to do.

Follow the instructions for each question carefully.

If you need to do working out, you can use any space on the page – do not use rough paper.

Marks

Some questions have a method box like this.

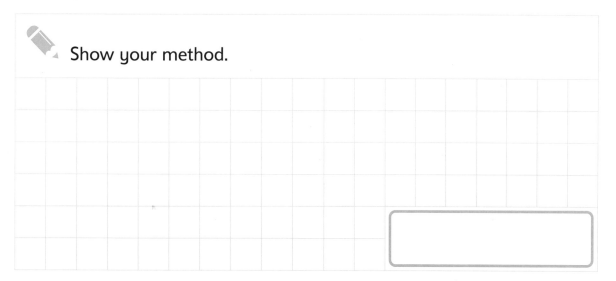

For these questions you may get a mark for showing your method.

The number on the right-hand side of the page tells you the maximum number of marks for each question.

1. Draw a circle around the smallest fraction.

$\dfrac{1}{7}$

$\dfrac{1}{8}$

$\dfrac{1}{9}$

Marks

1

Marks

2. This pictogram shows a survey of cars in a school car park.

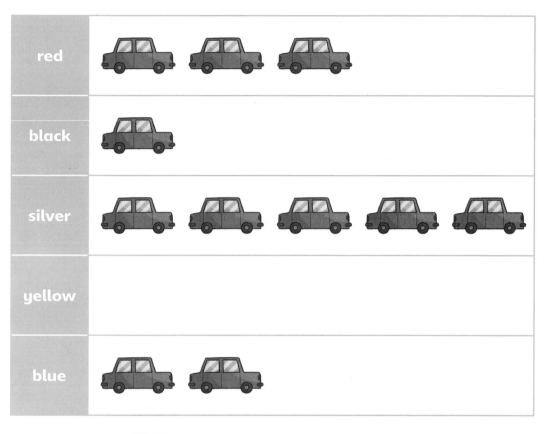

= 2 cars

How many cars were counted altogether?

1

How many more silver than black cars were there?

1

Marks

3. What number is 35 less than 60?

1

4. Count back 5 from 3.

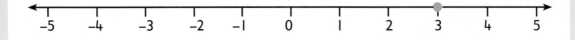

1

SCHOLASTIC National Curriculum SATs Tests

Marks

5. Write the two missing digits to make this multiplication correct.

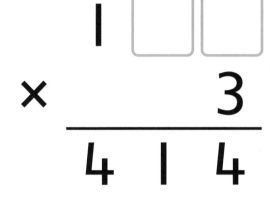

2

6. Write the number 5304 in words.

_____

_____

1

Marks

7. Tanya and her little brother each want a comic.

Tanya wants *Bingo*, and her brother wants *Elfworld*.

Bingo

£2.45

Elfworld
£2.00

How much change would they have left from a £5 note?

✎ Show your method.

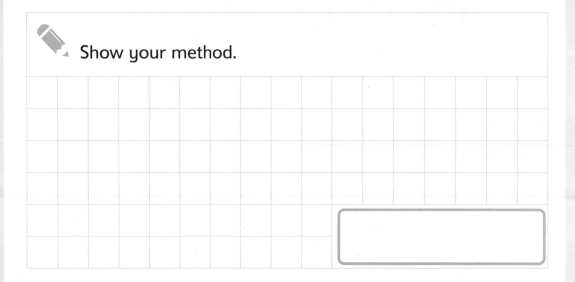

2

How much would three copies of Bingo cost?

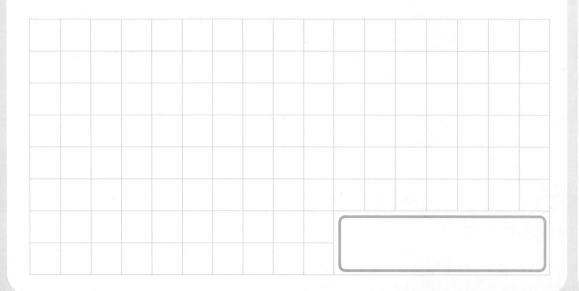

1

30

8. Round each of these decimals to the nearest whole number.

Marks

2.7

8.5

5.4

1

9. Roberta makes patterns stacking dice.

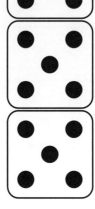

How many dots will there be on the fourth stack?

1

Marks

10. Complete the chart.

1000 less	Number	1000 more
1325	2325	3325
	8265	
	4037	
	5005	
	1000	

1

11. How many millimetres are there in $5\frac{1}{2}$ metres?
Circle the correct answer.

505   550   5050   5500   50500

1

Marks

12. The village of Diptoes is divided by a stream.

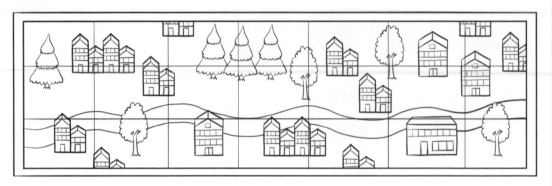

975 people live on the north side of the stream.

1408 people live on the south side of the stream.

What is the total population of the village?

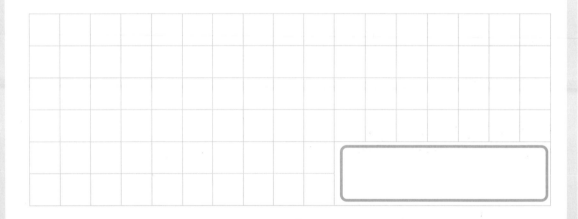

1

How many more people live on the south side of the village than on the north side?

1

13. Draw a line from each name to the correct triangle.

Marks

equilateral

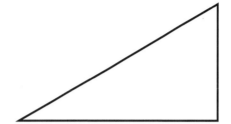

isosceles

right-angled

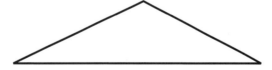

scalene

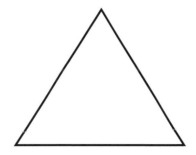

1

14. 500 letters are shared equally between five people to deliver them.

How many letters does each person have to deliver?

| letters |

Marks

1

3500 sacks of mail are divided equally into five delivery vans.

How many sacks go into each van?

| sacks |

1

SCHOLASTIC National Curriculum SATs Tests

Marks

15. Julian keeps a note of the time taken for different parts of a trip to the seaside.

Part of trip	Time taken
Bus ride to the train station	17 minutes
Waiting at the station	15 minutes
Train ride to the seaside	1 hour 24 minutes

How long does the journey take altogether? Give your answer in hours and minutes.

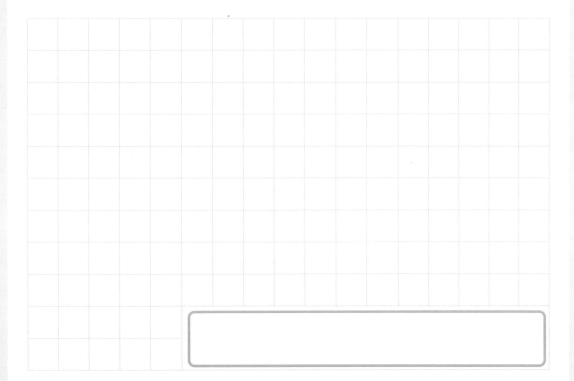

1

Julian started his journey at 10:30am. What time did he arrive at the seaside?

1

16.

20cm

height

The height of this rectangle is half as long as the length.

Calculate the perimeter.

cm

1

Marks

17.   Kevin thinks of two numbers. He says:

> If you add the numbers together you get 16. If you multiply them together, you get 15.

What are the two numbers?

_____ and _____

1

18. Plot these points on the coordinate grid below.

Marks

A (2, 3)   B (6, 4)   C (5, 8)

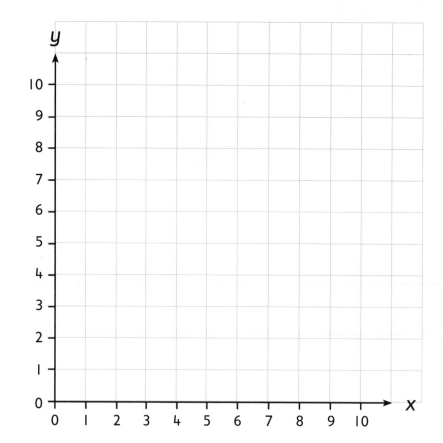

1

Mark on the grid the point D, so that ABCD is a square.

1

Write the coordinates of point D.

(____ , ____)

1

Marks

19. Write the missing numbers in the spaces to make this subtraction correct.

$$
\begin{array}{r}
4\ 3\ 2\ 5 \\
-\ 1\ \boxed{}\ \boxed{}\ 8 \\
\hline
2\ 5\ 1\ 7
\end{array}
$$

1

20. A shop sells soft toys.

Six small cuddly rabbits cost £15.

What is the cost of one rabbit?

Marks

Show your method.

£

2

SCHOLASTIC National Curriculum SATs Tests

21. Ahmet says that 47 × 23 = 1325.

Eve says that he is wrong. She can tell without repeating the whole calculation.

Explain how Eve knows.

_____

_____

_____

_____

_____

1

22. There are 160 people in a cinema.

$\frac{3}{8}$ of them are children.

How many children are in the cinema?

Marks

children

1

SCHOLASTIC National Curriculum SATs Tests

23. A wooden plank is 2.5 metres long.

How long would 12 planks be laid end to end?

1

24. A builder needs 125 bricks and two sacks of cement to build a small wall.

Marks

How much will it cost altogether?

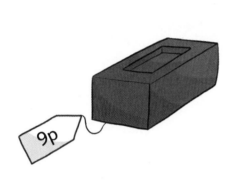

9p

bag of cement £5.50

✏ Show your method.

2

Q	Strand	Sub-strand	Possible marks	Actual marks
1	Fractions, decimals and percentages	Comparing and ordering fractions	1	
2	Statistics	Solve problems involving data	2	
3	Calculations	Add and subtract mentally	1	
4	Number and place value	Negative numbers	1	
5	Calculations	Multiply using written methods	2	
6	Number and place value	Read and write numbers	1	
7	Measurement	Solve problems involving money	3	
8	Fractions, decimals and percentages	Rounding decimals	1	
9	Number and place value	Counting (in multiples)	1	
10	Number and place value	Place value	1	
11	Measurement	Convert between metric units	1	
12	Calculations	Add and subtract using written methods	2	
13	Geometry – properties of shapes	Describe properties and classify shapes	1	
14	Calculations	Use place value, known and derived facts to multiply and divide mentally	2	
15	Measurement	Solve problems involving time	2	
16	Measurement	Calculate perimeter	1	
17	Number and place value	Solving number problems	1	
18	Geometry – position and direction	Describe positions on a 2D grid as coordinates	3	
19	Calculations	Add and subtract using written methods	1	
20	Calculations	Solve problems involving all four operations	2	
21	Calculations	Estimate, use inverses and check	1	
22	Fractions, decimals and percentages	Solve problems involving non-unit fractions to calculate quantities	1	
23	Measurement	Solve problems involving length	1	
24	Calculations	Multiply using written methods	2	
		Total	35	

Instructions Test A: Paper 3

- You have **40 minutes** for this test paper.
- You may **not use** a calculator to answer any questions in this test paper.
- Work as quickly and carefully as you can.
- Try to answer all the questions. If you cannot do one of the questions, **go on to the next one**. You can come back to it later, if you have time.
- If you finish before the end, **go back and check your work**.
- Ask your teacher if you are not sure what to do.

Follow the instructions for each question carefully.

If you need to do working out, you can use any space on the page – do not use rough paper.

Marks

Some questions have a method box like this.

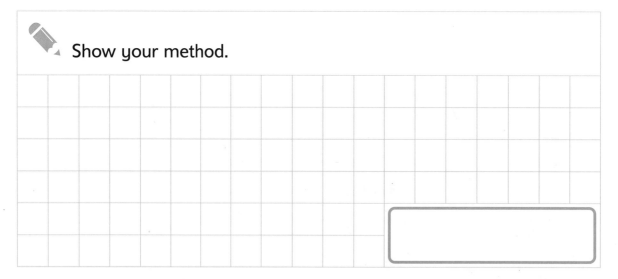

Show your method.

For these questions you may get a mark for showing your method.

The number on the right-hand side of the page tells you the maximum number of marks for each question.

Marks

1. Write each of these decimals on its correct place on the number line.

0.2   0.6   0.9

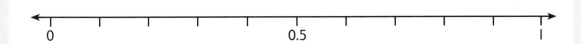

0   0.5   1

1

2. The first three numbers are missing from this sequence.

Fill in the gaps to complete the sequence.

$\boxed{}$, $\boxed{}$, $\boxed{}$, 36, 42, 48

Marks

1

SCHOLASTIC National Curriculum SATs Tests

3.

2389 − 1468 = 921 ✔

Mark each of these calculations with a ✔ or ✘.

2389 + 921 = 1468 ☐

2389 − 921 = 1468 ☐

1468 + 921 = 2389 ☐

1468 − 921 = 2389 ☐

Marks

1

Marks

4. Write the missing numbers in the boxes.

$$
\begin{array}{r}
8\ 7\ 5 \\
+\ \ 3\ \square\ \square \\
\hline
1\ 2\ 3\ 4
\end{array}
$$

1

5. Gemma had a box of 24 chocolates. She ate two of them and kindly gave three to her mum, three to her dad, two to her sister and one to her brother.

How many chocolates were left?

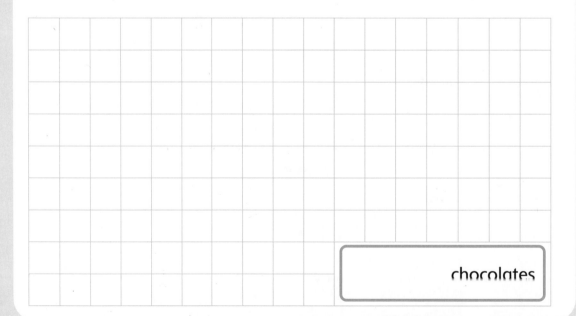

chocolates

1

SCHOLASTIC National Curriculum SATs Tests

Marks

6. A newborn baby weighs four kilograms.

Write the baby's weight in grams.

g

1

A toddler is one metre tall.

Write her height in centimetres.

cm

1

7. Write the decimal equivalent to each fraction.

Marks

$\frac{1}{4}$ =

$\frac{1}{2}$ =

$\frac{3}{4}$ =

1

8. Eight children each give 85p to raise money for charity.

How much will they collect altogether?

✏ Show your method.

Marks

2

9. Write this number in digits.

three thousand and eighty-five

1

In the number 345, the digit 3 represents three hundreds.

What does the digit 4 represent in each of these numbers?

124 _____

3482 _____

2042 _____

1

Write the largest 4-digit number that can be made with the digits 0, 1, 2 and 3. Use each digit only once.

1

Marks

10. In a class experiment, the teacher heated a beaker of ice until it turned to water and boiled.

This graph shows how the temperature of the water increased.

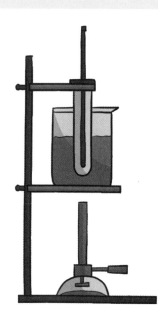

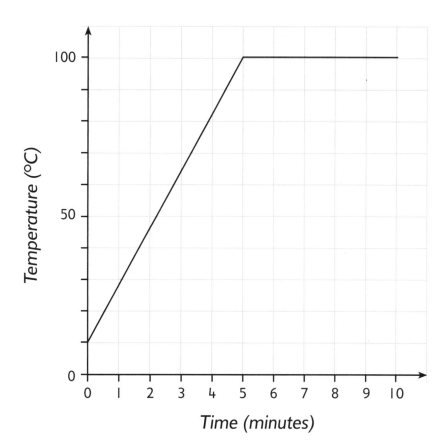

Time (minutes)

How long did it take to heat the water to 100°C?

minutes

1

11. In a class of 30 children, a survey of pets shows that seven children own a dog, six own a cat, and four own a guinea pig.

What fraction of the class own a pet?

1

What fraction of the class do not own a pet?

1

Marks

12. A builder orders 4000 bricks to build a wall, but only uses 2844.

How many bricks are left over?

bricks

1

13. Draw lines to join each word to the correct decimal.

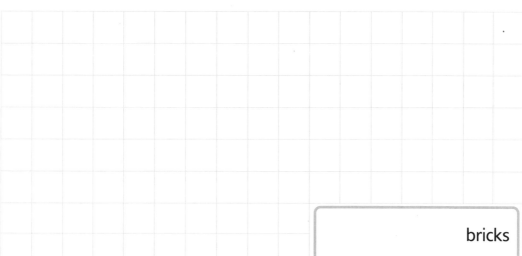

five-tenths	0.05
three-hundredths	0.5
zero point zero five	0.3
zero point three	0.03

1

14. Tina visits a fruit shop.

She can buy 12 apples for the same cost as eight bananas.

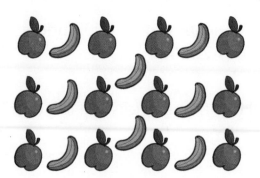

Marks

If one apple costs 6p, how much does one banana cost?

✎ Show your method.

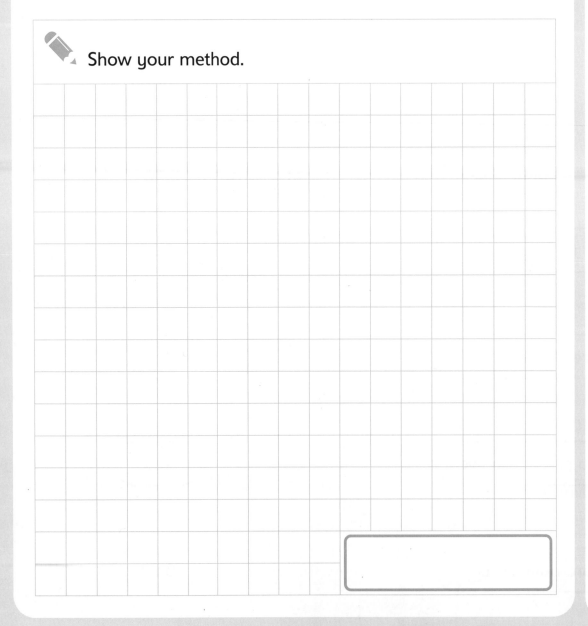

3

Marks

15. Write the correct angle name in each box.

acute   obtuse   right angle

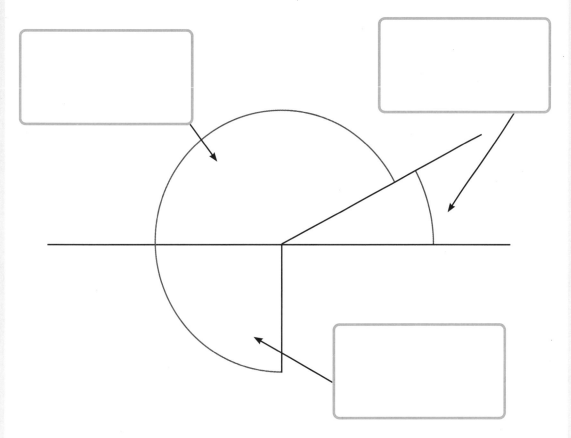

1

16. Circle the correct value for these Roman numerals.

XCVI

26   56   96   116

1

Marks

17. An aeroplane can carry up to 100 passengers.

When the plane is one-quarter full, how many passengers are there?

1

On Sunday, there were 35 adults and 37 children on board.

What fraction of the seats were empty?

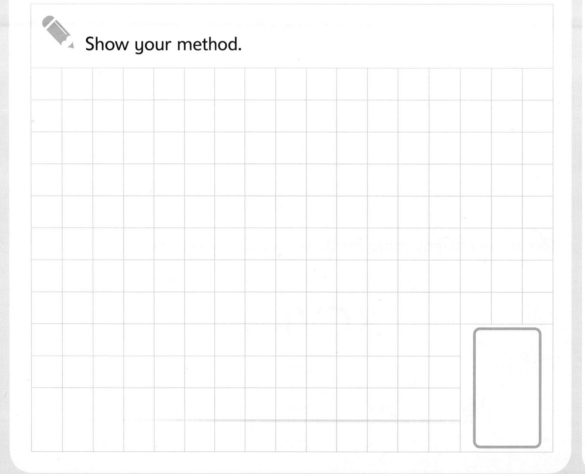

Show your method.

2

■SCHOLASTIC National Curriculum SATs Tests

18.

Six people share a winning lottery ticket. Altogether they receive £4800. They share the money equally.

How much do they each receive?

£

1

19. A jug holds exactly 1 litre of juice, and paper party cups hold 300 millilitres.

Marks

How many cups can be filled from the jug?

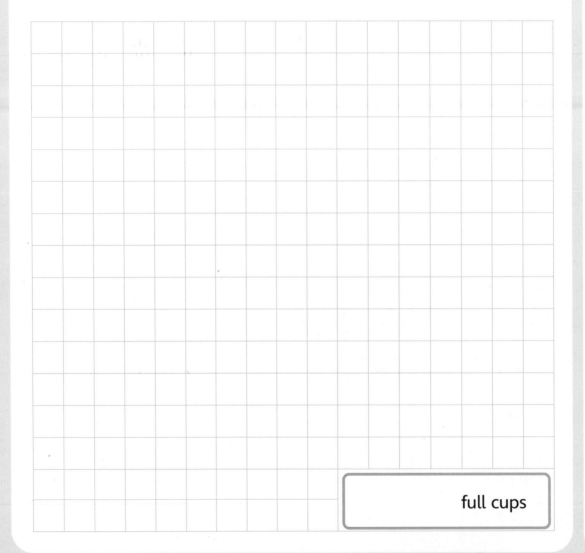

full cups

1

20. These are the numbers of children in each year group of a junior school.

Marks

Year 3	Year 4	Year 5	Year 6
50	55	48	59

How many children are there altogether in the school?

1

The greatest number of children allowed in the school is 240.

How many spare places are there in the school?

1

21. Kerry takes 4 pieces of wood and arranges them in a rectangle. Each piece of wood is 140cm long and 35cm wide.

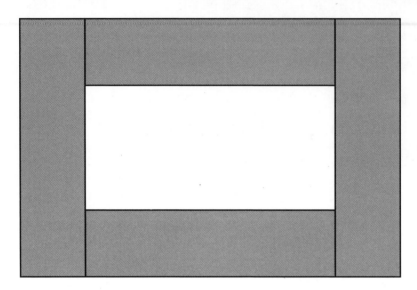

Find the perimeter of the outside of the shape.

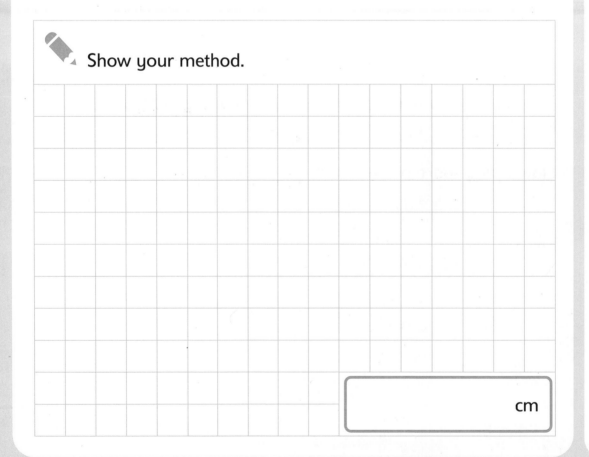

Show your method.

cm

2

22. Translate the square ABCD by two squares right and three squares up.

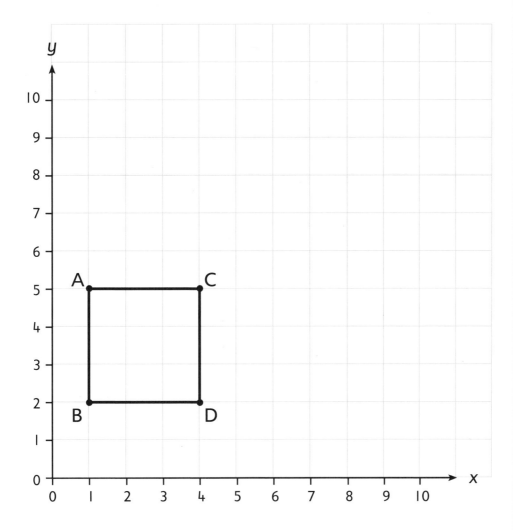

1

23. What is half of one-eighth?

Marks

1

SCHOLASTIC National Curriculum SATs Tests

24. Molly makes a shape using four identical squares.

Use a ruler to draw lines of symmetry of the shape.

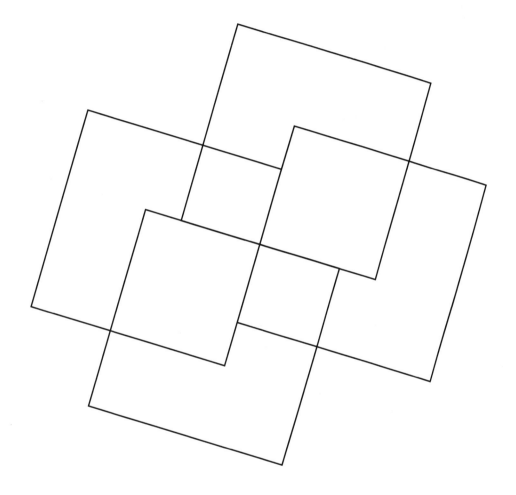

Test A: Paper 3 Marks

Q	Strand	Sub-strand	Possible marks	Actual marks
1	Fractions, decimals, percentages	Comparing decimals	1	
2	Number and place value	Counting (in multiples)	1	
3	Calculations	Estimate, use inverses and check	1	
4	Calculations	Add and subtract using written methods	1	
5	Calculations	Solving problems involving addition and subtraction	1	
6	Measurement	Convert metric units	2	
7	Fractions, decimals and percentages	Equivalence of fractions and decimals	1	
8	Calculations	Multiply using written methods	2	
9	Number and place value	Read, write, order and compare numbers; recognise the place value of digits	3	
10	Statistics	Interpret and represent data	1	
11	Fractions, decimals, percentages	Solve problems involving increasingly harder fractions	2	
12	Calculations	Add and subtract using written methods	1	
13	Fractions, decimals and percentages	Equivalence of decimals and tenths and hundredths	1	
14	Calculations	Solve problems involving all four operations	3	
15	Geometry – properties of shapes	Identify acute angles, obtuse angles and right angles	1	
16	Number and place value	Roman numerals	1	
17	Fractions, decimals, percentages	Solve problems involving fractions to calculate quantities; write fractions	3	
18	Calculations	Use place value, known and derived facts to multiply and divide mentally	1	
19	Measurement	Solve problems involving capacity	1	
20	Calculations	Add and subtract to solve problems	2	
21	Measurement	Calculate perimeter	2	
22	Geometry – position and direction	Describe position, direction and movement	1	
23	Fractions, decimals, percentages	Solve problems involving increasingly harder fractions	1	
24	Geometry – properties of shapes	Describe properties and classify shapes	1	
		Total	35	

Instructions Test B: Paper 1

You **may not** use a calculator to answer any questions in this test.

Questions and answers

- You have **30 minutes** to complete this test.
- Work as quickly and carefully as you can.
- Put your answer in the box for each question.

- If you cannot do one of the questions, **go on to the next one**. You can come back to it later if you have time.
- If you finish before the end, **go back and check your work**.

Marks

- The number next to each box at the side of the page tells you the maximum number of marks for each question.
- In this test, short division and long multiplication questions are worth **2 marks** each. You will be awarded 2 marks for a correct answer.
- You may get 1 mark for showing a formal method.

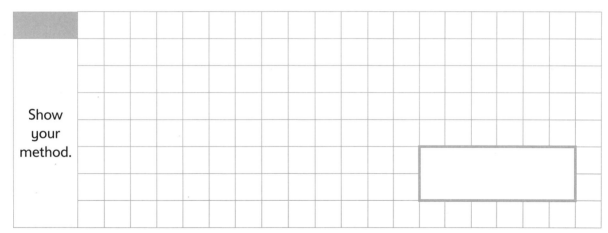

- All other questions are worth **1 mark** each.

1. 36 − 7 =

Marks

1

2. $\frac{1}{2}$ of 12 =

1

3. 5 × 7 =

1

Marks

4. 13 + 9 =

1

5. 1000 − 300 =

1

6. 87 − 45 =

1

7. 47 + 200 =

Marks

1

8. 50 × 10 =

1

9. 63 ÷ 10 =

1

SCHOLASTIC National Curriculum SATs Tests

Marks

10.   0.1 + 0.1 + 0.1 =

1

11.

```
    3 2 2
    1 0 5
  + 2 5 1
  _____
```

1

12.   3 × 5 + 3 × 7 =

1

13. 684 + 4000 =

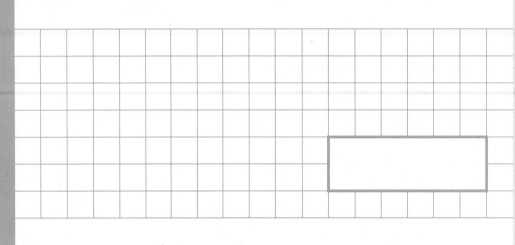

Marks

1

14. $1 - \frac{2}{5} =$

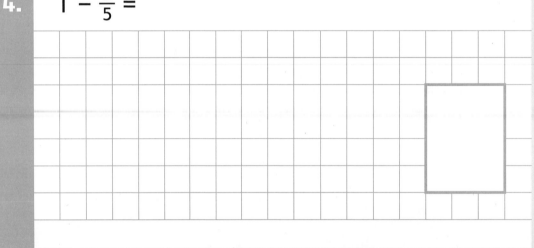

1

15. 3562 × 1 =

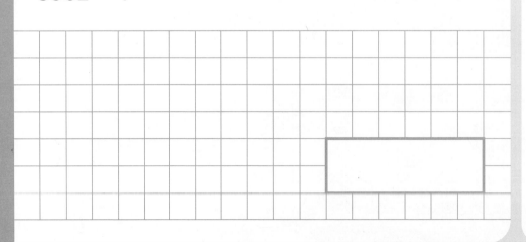

1

Marks

16. $\dfrac{8}{12} - \dfrac{3}{12} =$

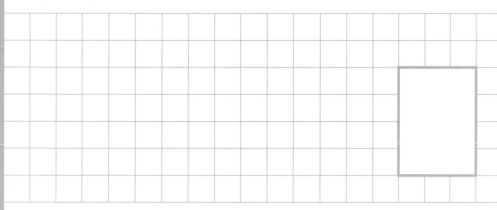

1

17. 275 + 103 =

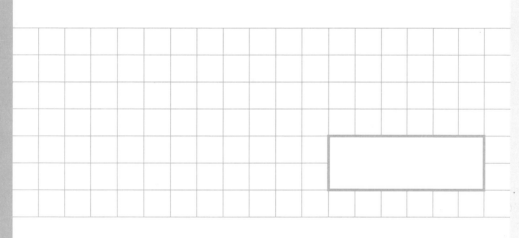

1

18. 9 + 9 + 9 + 9 + 9 + 9 =

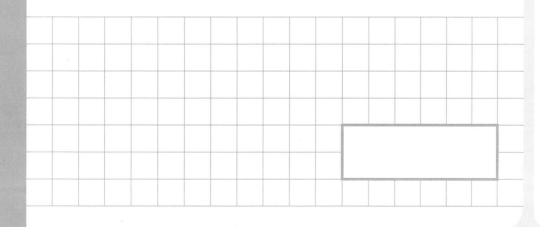

1

19. 2375 − 300 =

Marks

1

20. 5600 − 3999 =

1

21. 800 × 5 =

1

SCHOLASTIC National Curriculum SATs Tests

22. 326 − _____ = 131

Marks

1

23. 3 × 5 × 5 =

1

24. 50 − 12 − 9 =

1

25.

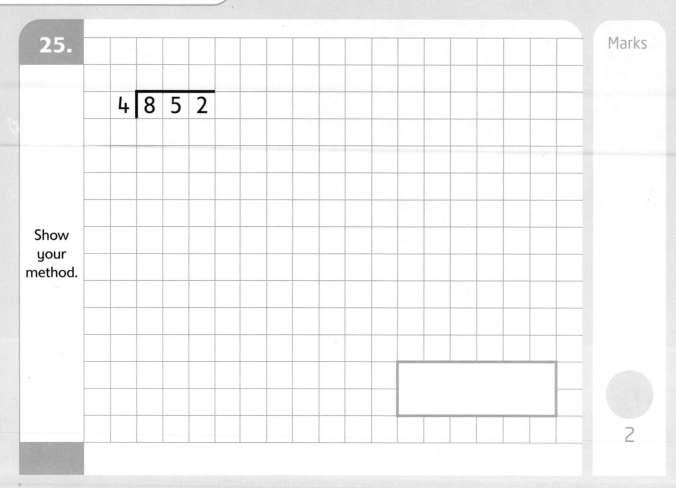

4) 8 5 2

Show your method.

Marks

2

26.

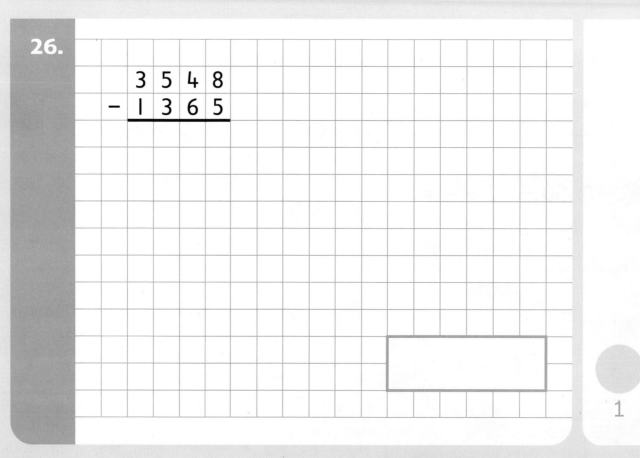

$$
\begin{array}{r}
3\ 5\ 4\ 8 \\
-\ 1\ 3\ 6\ 5 \\
\hline
\end{array}
$$

Marks

1

27. $\frac{1}{4}$ of 500 =

Marks

1

28.

```
   4 7 8 6
 + 3 0 7 6
 ─────────
```

1

29. 55 × 3 =

1

30. $\frac{1}{4} + \frac{1}{4} + \frac{1}{4} =$

1

31. $325 \times 3 =$

Show your method.

2

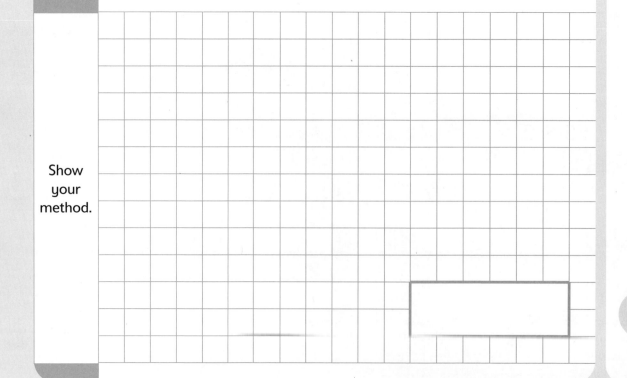

32. $25 \div 100 =$

Marks

1

33.

	2	7	3
×			5

Show your method.

2

34. 3865 + 3000 − 2000 =

Marks

1

35. $\frac{2}{3}$ of 360 =

1

36.

Show your method.

5) 6 7 1

2

Q	Strand	Possible marks	Actual marks
1	36 – 7	1	
2	$\frac{1}{2}$ of 12	1	
3	5 × 7	1	
4	13 + 9	1	
5	1000 – 300	1	
6	87 – 45	1	
7	47 + 200	1	
8	50 × 10	1	
9	63 ÷ 10	1	
10	0.1 + 0.1 + 0.1	1	
11	3 2 2 1 0 5 + 2 5 1	1	
12	3 × 5 + 3 × 7	1	
13	684 + 4000	1	
14	$1 - \frac{2}{5}$	1	
15	3562 × 1	1	
16	$\frac{8}{12} - \frac{3}{12}$	1	
17	275 + 103	1	
18	9 + 9 + 9 + 9 + 9 + 9	1	

Q	Strand	Possible marks	Actual marks
19	2375 – 300	1	
20	5600 – 3999	1	
21	800 × 5	1	
22	326 – ____ = 131	1	
23	3 × 5 × 5	1	
24	50 – 12 – 9	1	
25	4 ⟌ 8 5 2	2	
26	3 5 4 8 – 1 3 6 5	1	
27	$\frac{1}{4}$ of 500	1	
28	4 7 8 6 + 3 0 7 6	1	
29	55 × 3	1	
30	$\frac{1}{4} + \frac{1}{4} + \frac{1}{4}$	1	
31	325 × 3	2	
32	25 ÷ 100	1	
33	2 7 3 × 5	2	
34	3865 + 3000 – 2000	1	
35	$\frac{2}{3}$ of 360	1	
36	5 ⟌ 6 7 1	2	
	Total	**40**	

Instructions Test B: Paper 2

- You have **40 minutes** for this test paper.
- You may **not use** a calculator to answer any questions in this test paper.
- Work as quickly and carefully as you can.
- Try to answer all the questions. If you cannot do one of the questions, **go on to the next one**. You can come back to it later, if you have time.
- If you finish before the end, **go back and check your work**.
- Ask your teacher if you are not sure what to do.

Follow the instructions for each question carefully.

If you need to do working out, you can use any space on the page – do not use rough paper.

Marks

Some questions have a method box like this.

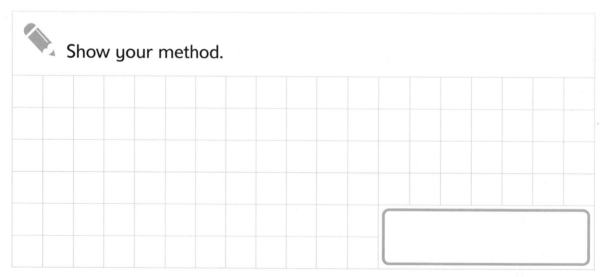

Show your method.

For these questions you may get a mark for showing your method.

The number on the right-hand side of the page tells you the maximum number of marks for each question.

1. Draw the next two shapes in this sequence.

Marks

1

2. Round 1.9 to the nearest whole number.

1

3. Tim has emptied all of the money from his piggy bank.

Marks

Which coin does Tim have most of?

1

How much does Tim have in his piggy bank?

1

Tim takes out 15p. How much is left in the piggy bank?

1

Marks

4. Complete the sequence.

70, 77, 84, ☐ , ☐ , ☐ , 112

1

5. In a class of 30 children: 15 have black hair, 10 have brown hair, and 5 have blonde hair.

Write the colour hair as a fraction of the whole class in the simplest form.

black hair ☐

brown hair ☐

blonde hair ☐

1

6. Write this number in numerals.

six thousand, seven hundred and forty-two

☐

1

7. Ben is comparing the length of different objects.

Number the objects from 1 to 5, with 1 for the shortest up to 5 for the longest.

The shortest has been done for you.

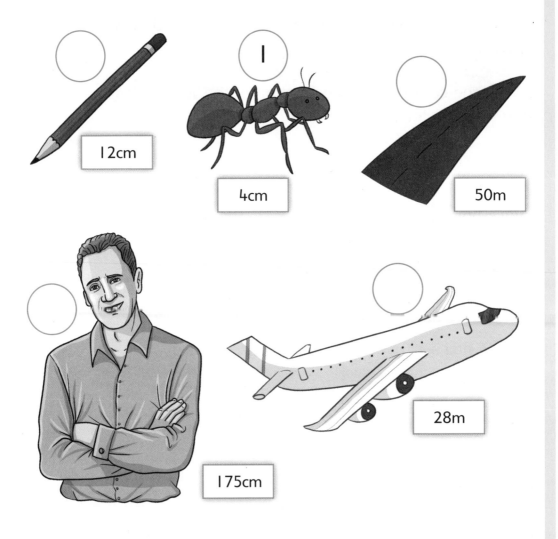

12cm

1

4cm

50m

175cm

28m

1

Write the height of Ben's dad in millimetres.

mm

1

8. Hennaz is picking blackberries. She already has 47, but eats 16 of them, so she collects some more. Eventually she has 85 blackberries.

How many **more** did she collect?

Marks

blackberries

1

9. Arrange these numbers in order, from smallest to largest.

| 1005 | 9555 | 999 | 5999 | 555 | 1009 |

_____

_____

_____

_____

_____

_____

1

10. Round each number to the nearest thousand.

Marks

6701

2498

5500

1

11. There are 7539 people at a football tournament.

If 3240 are adults, how many children are there at the match?

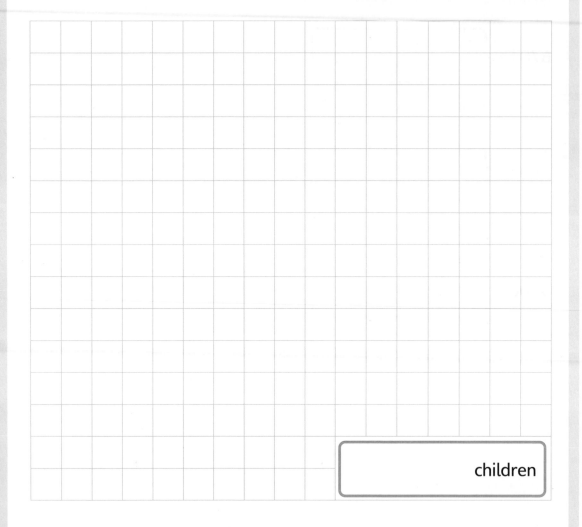

children

1

Marks

12. Two straight lines cross and make four angles: two acute, and two obtuse.

Complete the chart with the name of each angle.

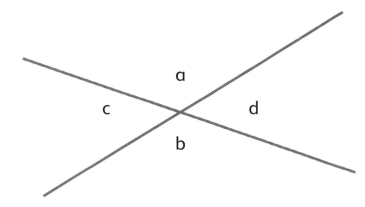

Angle	a	b	c	d
Acute or obtuse				

1

Explain what an acute angle is.

_____

_____

_____

_____

1

13. A train begins a journey of 250 miles.

The train stops after 135 miles.

How far does it still have to travel?

Marks

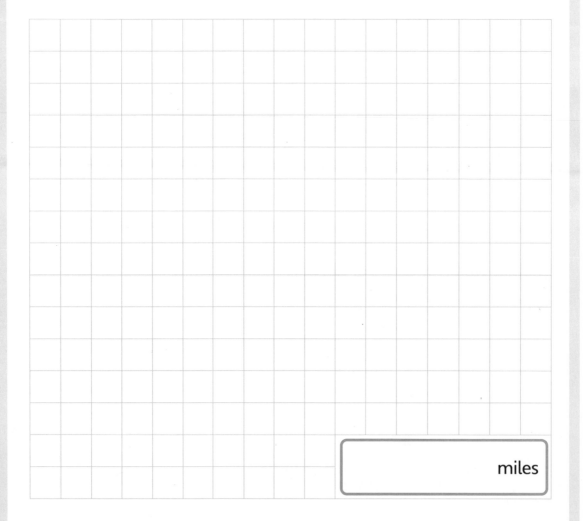

miles

1

Marks

14. How many legs do 236 chairs have altogether? Each chair has four legs.

Show your method.

legs

2

15. Complete the square ABCD on the coordinate grid below.

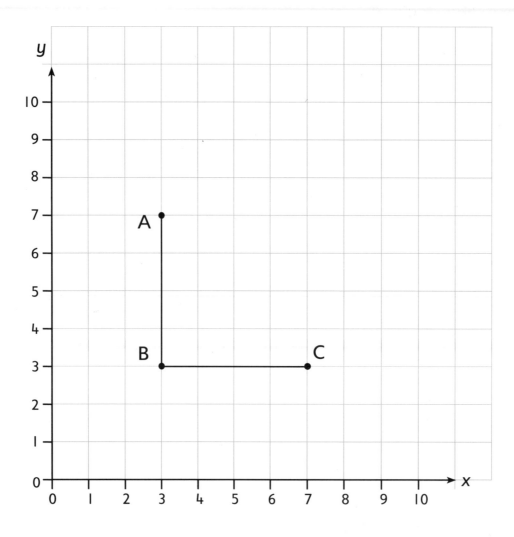

1

Write the coordinates for vertex D.

(_____ , _____)

1

The centre of the square has coordinates (5, 5). On the coordinate grid, plot the centre with a cross.

1

16. One quarter of twenty-eight children have ginger coloured hair.

How many children is that?

Marks

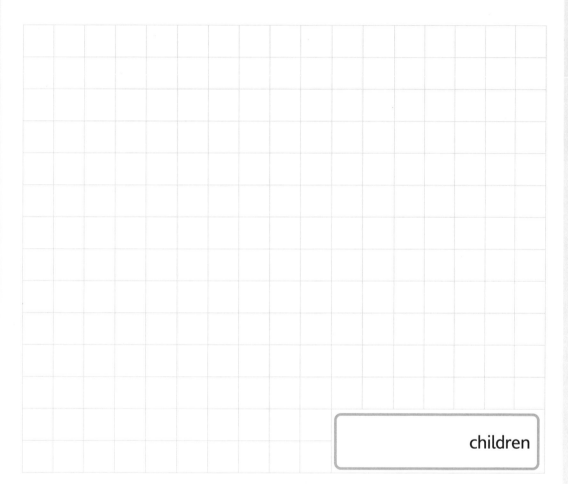

| | children |

1

17. Jenny and her mum are waiting to catch a bus.

Marks

What is the time? Draw the hands on the clock face.

The bus will leave at twenty past three in the afternoon.

How long must Jenny and her mum wait for the bus to leave?

1

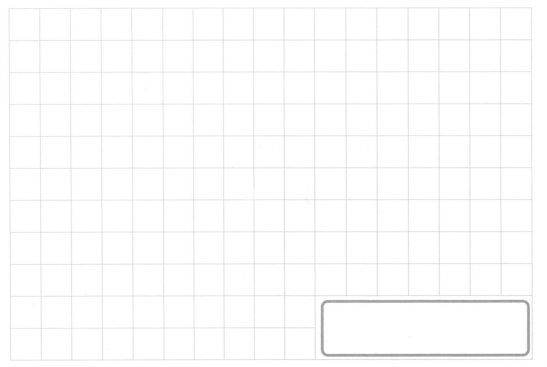

1

Marks

18. Six cinema tickets cost £24 altogether.

How much do four tickets cost?

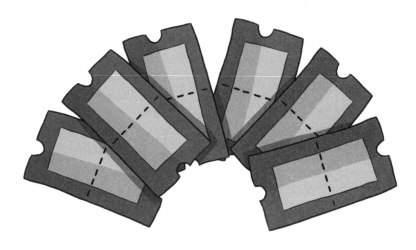

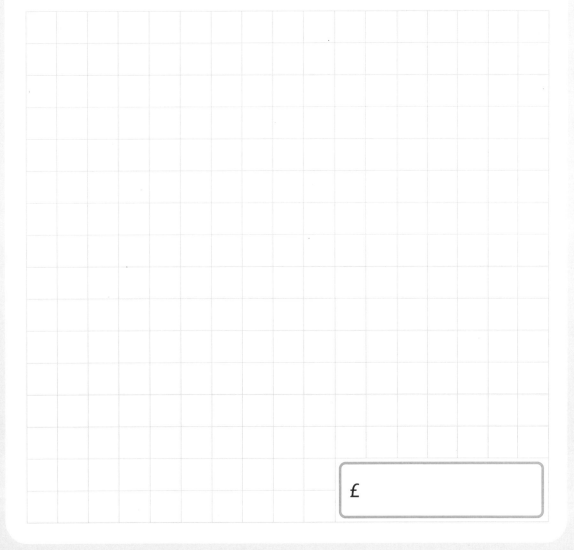

£

1

19. This shape is a rhombus.

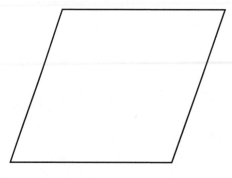

Marks

Put a tick next to each TRUE statement.

All sides are the same length. ☐

All the angles are equal. ☐

Opposite sides are parallel. ☐

All angles are right angles. ☐

There are no parallel sides. ☐

Opposite angles are equal. ☐

1

 National Curriculum SATs Tests

20. Chen has one orange.

She eats three-quarters of the orange.

How much orange is left?

Marks

1

Robert eats one-fifth of a bag of apples.

He ate two apples.

How many apples were in the bag when it was full?

apples

1

21. Write the missing numbers in the boxes.

$$
\begin{array}{r}
1\ 5\ 4\ 3 \\
-\quad \square\ 1\ \square \\
\hline
8\ 2\ 5
\end{array}
$$

1

22. 435 birds land in equal groups in five trees.

How many birds are in each tree?

Marks

Show your method.

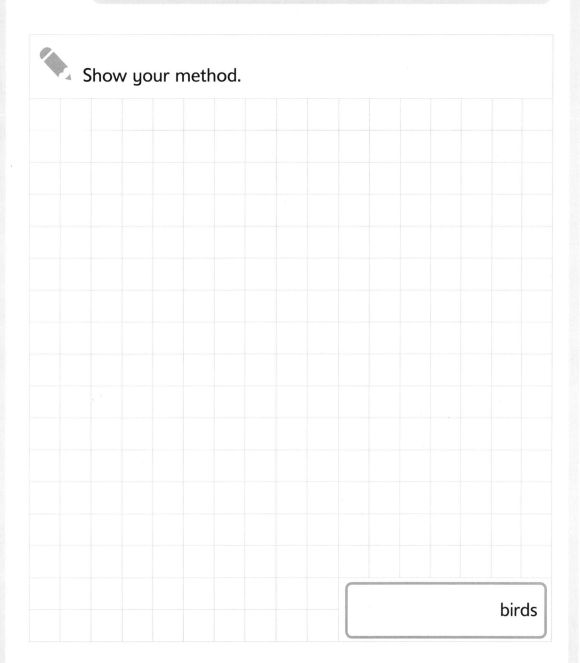

birds

2

Marks

23. Football shirts cost £27.

The price is reduced by half in a sale.

Calculate the sale price.

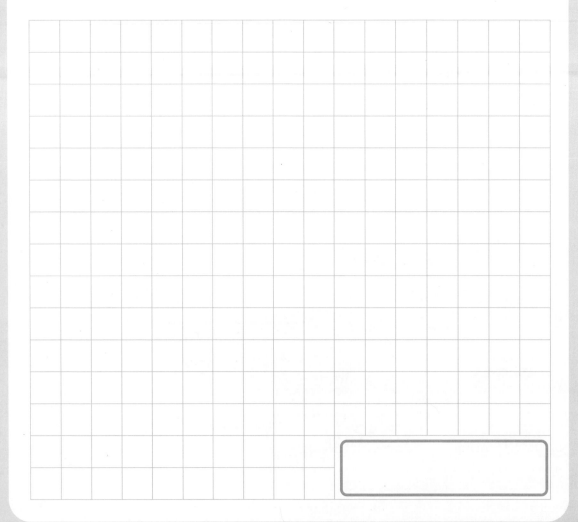

1

SCHOLASTIC National Curriculum SATs Tests

Marks

24. The graph shows the temperature in a garden for 24 hours.

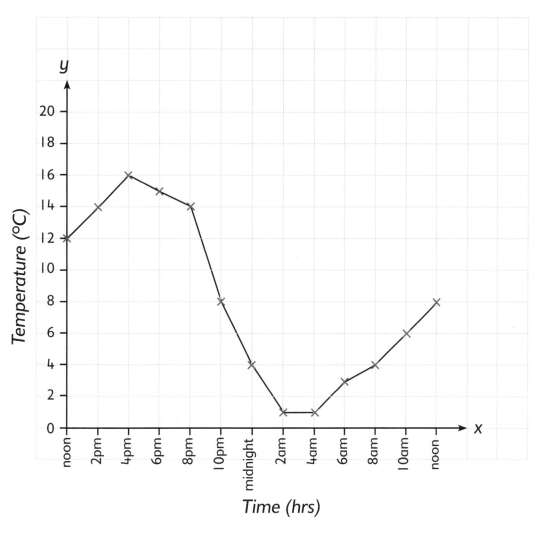

When was the temperature hottest?

1

Write the two times when the temperature was 6°C.

_____ and _____

1

Q	Strand	Sub-strand	Possible marks	Actual marks
1	Geometry – position and direction	Patterns	1	
2	Fractions, decimals and percentages	Rounding decimals	1	
3	Measurement	Solving problems involving money	3	
4	Number and place value	Counting (in multiples)	1	
5	Fractions, decimals and percentages	Solve problems involving fractions to calculate quantities	1	
6	Number and place value	Read, write, order and compare numbers	1	
7	Measurement	Compare lengths; convert between metric units	2	
8	Calculations	Add and subtract	1	
9	Number and place value	Compare and order numbers	1	
10	Number and place value	Identify, represent and estimate; rounding	1	
11	Calculations	Subtract using written methods	1	
12	Geometry – properties of shapes	Identify acute angles, obtuse angles and right angles	2	
13	Calculations	Solve problems involving addition and subtraction	1	
14	Calculations	Multiply using written methods	2	
15	Geometry – position and direction	Describe positions on a 2D grid as coordinates	3	
16	Fractions, decimals and percentages	Solve problems involving fractions to calculate quantities	1	
17	Measurement	Telling time; calculating duration	2	
18	Calculations	Solve integer scaling problems	1	
19	Geometry – properties of shapes	Describe properties and classify shapes	1	
20	Fractions, decimals and percentages	Add and subtract fractions; solve problems involving fractions	2	
21	Calculations	Estimate, use inverses and check	1	
22	Calculations	Divide using written methods	2	
23	Fractions, decimals and percentages	Solve money problems involving fractions and decimals	1	
24	Statistics	Solve problems involving data	2	
		Total	**35**	

Instructions Test B: Paper 3

- You have **40 minutes** for this test paper.
- You may **not use** a calculator to answer any questions in this test paper.
- Work as quickly and carefully as you can.
- Try to answer all the questions. If you cannot do one of the questions, **go on to the next one**. You can come back to it later, if you have time.
- If you finish before the end, **go back and check your work**.
- Ask your teacher if you are not sure what to do.

Follow the instructions for each question carefully.

If you need to do working out, you can use any space on the page – do not use rough paper.

Marks

Some questions have a method box like this.

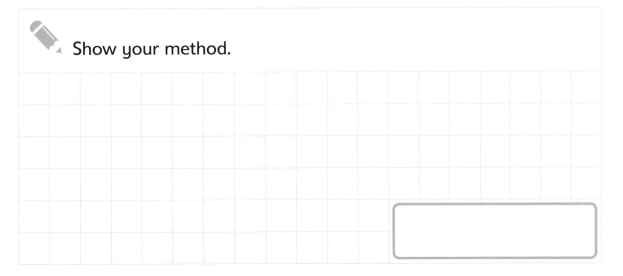

For these questions you may get a mark for showing your method.

The number on the right-hand side of the page tells you the maximum number of marks for each question.

I. A pattern is made by repeating two shapes.

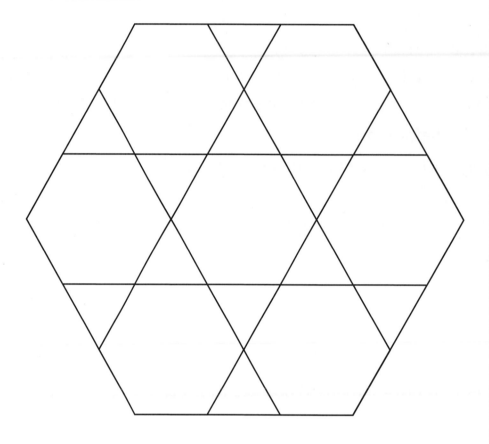

Shade one example of each shape.

1

Write the name of each shapes.

_____

_____

1

2. Write these decimals in order, from smallest to largest.

Marks

0.99   1.0   1.1   0.9   0.91

1

3. Round each decimal to the nearest whole number.

0.9 ☐

6.5 ☐

8.3 ☐

Marks

1

SCHOLASTIC National Curriculum SATs Tests

4. Tina buys two books.

She gives the shop assistant £15.

Marks

£8.99   £5.99

How much change will she receive?

✎ Show your method.

2

£3.50

Tina would like to buy a pad and pen.

Tina receives 50p pocket money each week.

How long will she have to save for?

1

5. A farmer has two square fields joined together.

She wants to put a fence around the perimeter of both fields.

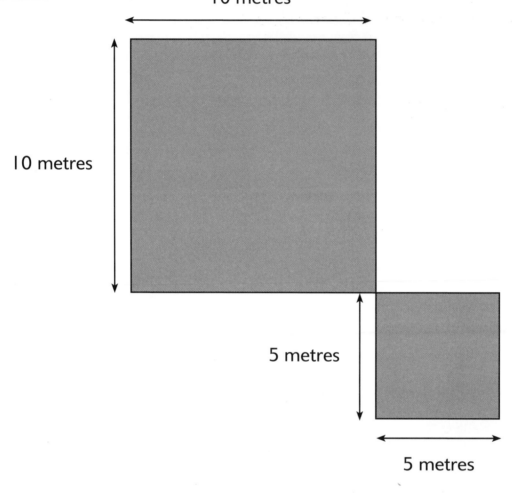

10 metres

10 metres

5 metres

5 metres

What will be the total length of the fences?

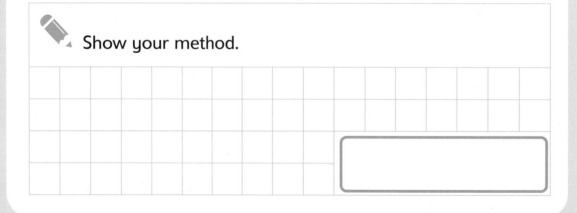

Show your method.

2

6. Arun starts at 7 and counts back 12.

Where will he stop?

Marks

1

7. Some cyclists ride for 48 miles a day for six days.

How far have they travelled altogether?

Marks

🖉 Show your method.

miles

2

8. Write 34 in Roman numerals.

Marks

1

Marks

9. Two children have been measuring the capacity of different containers.

Mug: 100 millilitres
Bottle: 1 litre
Vase: 115 millilitres
Egg cup: 23 millilitres

Write the capacity of the bottle in millilitres.

ml

1

Write the object names in order, from the smallest capacity to the largest capacity.

Smallest →			Largest

1

How many times could the bottle of water be used to fill the mug?

1

Marks

10. Find the missing number.

5 × _____ × 4 = 60

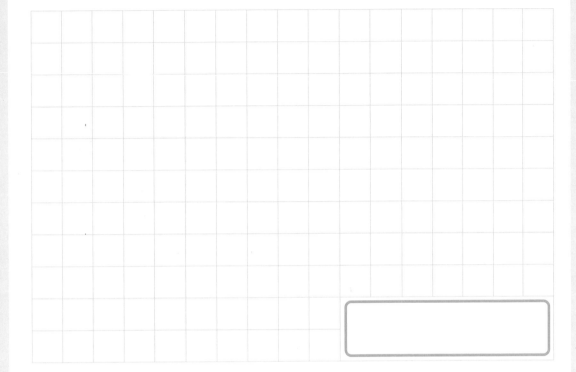

1

11. What does the digit 8 represent in this number?

4,204,837

Marks

1

12. A maths lesson lasts 45 minutes.

How long is that in seconds?

Show your method.

Marks

seconds

2

Marks

13. Sort these shapes by writing their names in the correct places in the table.

rectangle

parallelogram

rhombus

square

	All sides equal	Opposite sides equal
All angles equal		
Opposite angles equal		

1

Name each of these quadrilaterals.

1

Marks

14. Find the difference between 3364 and 4575.

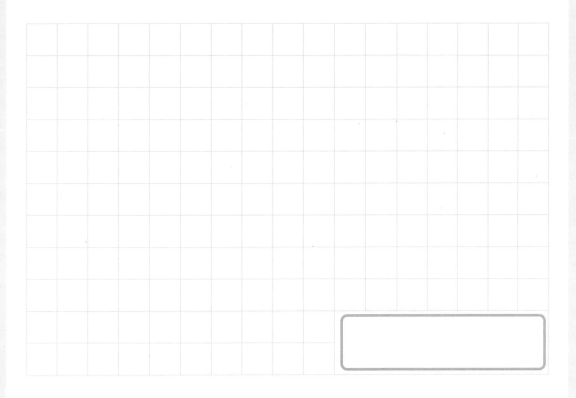

1

Find the sum of 3364 and 4575.

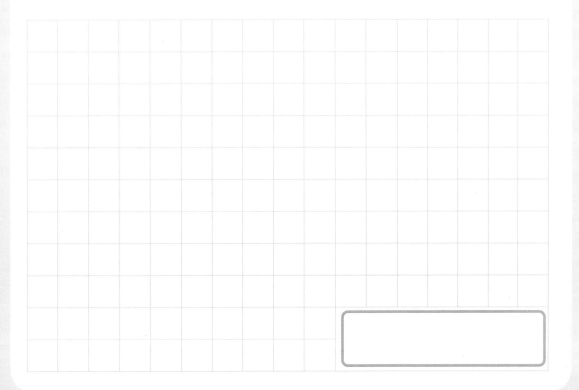

1

15. Circle the correct answer.

$43 \div 100 =$

Marks

4.3   0.43   0.043   0.0043

1

SCHOLASTIC National Curriculum SATs Tests

16. Draw a line to match each angle to its name.

Marks

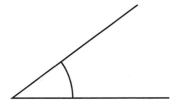

acute

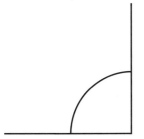

obtuse

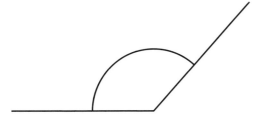

right angle

1

17. Circle the largest amount.

Marks

$\frac{1}{4}$ of 72 $\frac{1}{2}$ of 38

1

In a class of 24 children, $\frac{3}{8}$ of the class have blue eyes.

What fraction of the class have eyes that are not blue?

1

Complete the chart to show the number of children who have blue eyes and how many do not.

Eye colour	Blue	Not blue
Children		

1

Marks

18. The pictogram shows a survey of the way people travel to work.

bicycle	☺☺☺☺☺☺☺☺☺☺☺☺☺☺
bus	☺☺☺☺☺☺☺☺☺☺☺☺☺☺☺☺☺☺ ☺☺☺
car	☺☺☺☺☺☺☺☺☺☺
walking	☺☺☺☺☺☺☺☺☺☺☺☺☺☺☺☺☺☺ ☺☺☺☺☺☺☺☺
train	☺☺☺☺☺☺☺☺☺☺

☺ = 500 people

Tick each statement that the data shows to be true.

Walking is the most popular form of travel. ☐

1000 people travel by car. ☐

Trains are the fastest transport. ☐

As many people walk or cycle as use the other types of transport. ☐

1

19. A football stadium has 9000 seats.

Marks

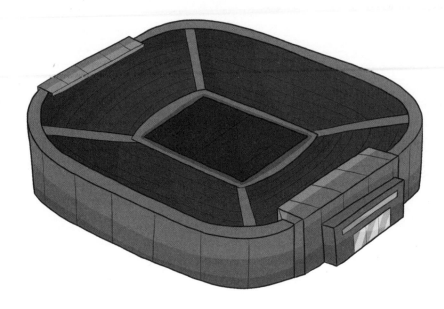

There is a match on Saturday, and 5435 tickets have been sold.

How many spare tickets are there?

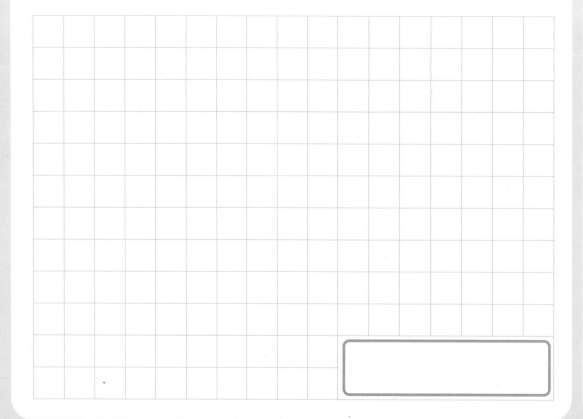

1

20. Complete these calculations.

Marks

75,356 + 42,871 = 118,227

118,227 − 75,356 =

1

118,227 − 42,871 =

1

21. A group of five adults win £9000 on the lottery.

They decide to give half of the money to charity and to share the rest between themselves.

lottery ticket

How much will each person receive?

Marks

✏ Show your method.

£

2

Q	Strand	Sub-strand	Possible marks	Actual marks
1	Geometry – properties of shapes	Recognise and name common shapes	2	
2	Fractions, decimals and percentages	Compare and order decimals	1	
3	Fractions, decimals and percentages	Rounding decimals	1	
4	Calculations	Solve problems involving money	3	
5	Measurement	Calculate perimeter	2	
6	Number and place value	Negative numbers	1	
7	Calculations	Multiply using written methods	2	
8	Number and place value	Roman numerals	1	
9	Measurement	Convert metric units; compare and order measures; solve problems involving capacity	3	
10	Calculations	Use place value, known and derived facts to multiply and divide mentally	1	
11	Number and place value	Place value	1	
12	Measurement	Solve problems involving units of time	2	
13	Geometry – properties of shapes	Describe properties and classify shapes	2	
14	Calculations	Add and subtract using written methods	2	
15	Fractions, decimals and percentages	Divide 1- and 2-digit numbers by 10 and 100	1	
16	Geometry – properties of shapes	Identify acute angles, obtuse angles and right angles	1	
17	Fractions, decimals, percentages	Solve problems involving fractions	3	
18	Statistics	Solve problems involving data	1	
19	Calculations	Solve problems involving subtraction	1	
20	Calculations	Solve problems involving commutative law and addition and subtraction	2	
21	Calculations	Use place value, known and derived facts to multiply and divide mentally	2	
		Total	**35**	

Marking and assessing the papers

The mark schemes provide details of correct answers including guidance for questions that have more than one mark.

Interpreting answers

The guidance below should be followed when deciding whether an answer is acceptable or not. As general guidance, answers should be unambiguous.

Problem	Guidance
The answer is equivalent to the one in the mark scheme.	The mark scheme will generally specify which equivalent responses are allowed. If this is not the case, award the mark unless the mark scheme states otherwise. For example: 1½ or 1.5
The answer is correct but the wrong working is shown.	A correct response will always be marked as correct.
The correct response has been crossed (or rubbed) out and not replaced.	Do not award the mark(s) for legible crossed-out answers that have not been replaced or that have been replaced by a further incorrect attempt.
The answer has been worked out correctly but an incorrect answer has been written in the answer box.	Where appropriate follow the guidance in the mark scheme. If no guidance is given then: ● award the mark if the incorrect answer is due to a transcription error ● award the mark if there is extra unnecessary workings which do not contradict work already done ● do not award the mark if there is extra unnecessary workings which do contradict work already done.
More than one answer is given.	If all answers are correct (or a range of answers is given, all of which are correct), the mark will be awarded unless specified otherwise by the mark schemes. If both correct and incorrect responses are given, no mark will be awarded.

■SCHOLASTIC National Curriculum SATs Tests

Problem	Guidance
There appears to be a misread of numbers affecting the working.	In general, the mark should not be awarded. However, in two-mark questions that have a working mark, award one mark if the working is applied correctly using the misread numbers, provided that the misread numbers are comparable in difficulty to the original numbers. For example, if '243' is misread as '234', both numbers may be regarded as comparable in difficulty.
No answer is given in the expected place, but the correct answer is given elsewhere.	Where an understanding of the question has been shown, award the mark. In particular, where a word or number response is expected, a pupil may meet the requirement by annotating a graph or labelling a diagram elsewhere in the question.

Formal written methods

The following guidance, showing examples of formal written methods, is taken directly from the National Curriculum guidelines. These methods may not be used in all schools and any formal written method, which is the preferred method of the school and which gives the correct answer, should be acceptable.

Short multiplication

24 × 6 becomes

```
      2   4
  ×       6
  1   4   4
      2
```

Answer: 144

342 × 7 becomes

```
    3   4   2
  ×         7
  2   3   9   4
      2   1
```

Answer: 2394

2741 × 6 becomes

```
    2   7   4   1
  ×             6
  1   6   4   4   6
          4   2
```

Answer: 16446

Short division

98 ÷ 7 becomes

```
      1   4
  7 | 9 ²8
```

Answer: 14

432 ÷ 5 becomes

```
        8   6   r2
  5 | 4   3  ³2
```

Answer: 86 remainder 2

496 ÷ 11 becomes

```
         4   5   r1
  11 | 4   9  ⁵6
```

Answer: $45\frac{1}{11}$

National standard in maths

The mark that your child gets in the test paper will be known as the 'raw score' (for example, '62' in 62/110). The raw score will be converted to a scaled score and children achieving a scaled score of 100 or more will achieve the national standard in that subject. These 'scaled scores' enable results to be reported consistently year-on-year.

The guidance in the table below shows the marks that children need to achieve to reach the national standard. This should be treated as a guide only, as the number of marks may vary. You can also find up-to-date information about scaled scores on our website: www.scholastic.co.uk/nationaltests

Total mark achieved	Standard
0–57	Has not met the national standard in mathematics for Year 4
58–110	Has met the national standard in mathematics for Year 4

Mark scheme Test A: Paper 1 (pages 10–24)

Q	Answers	Marks
1	3	1
2	15	1
3	28	1
4	4	1
5	4135	1
6	21	1
7	800	1
8	$\frac{2}{7}$	1
9	55	1
10	35	1
11	213	1
12	3300	1
13	93	1
14	0.2	1
15	$\frac{5}{6}$	1
16	200	1
17	9	1
18	5.4	1
19	3375	1
20	1440	1
21	373	1
22	6300	1
23	$\frac{5}{8}$	1
24	99	1
25	200	1
26	2616 Award 1 mark for a correct written method for short multiplication but with one arithmetic error.	2
27	0.03	1

■SCHOLASTIC National Curriculum SATs Tests

Q	Answers	Marks
28	142 Award 1 mark for a correct written method for short division but with one arithmetic error.	2
29	60	1
30	2691	1
31	4386	1
32	5300 Award 1 mark for a correct written method for short multiplication but with one arithmetic error.	2
33	9861	1
34	18	1
35	4671	1
36	273 r1 Award 1 mark for a correct written method for short division but with one arithmetic error.	2
	Total	**40**

Q	Answers	Marks
1	$\frac{1}{9}$	1
2	22	1
	8	1
3	25	1
4	−2	1
5	$\begin{array}{r} 1\,3\,8 \\ \times\quad 3 \\ \hline 4\,1\,4 \end{array}$ Award 1 mark if only one answer is correct.	2
6	Five thousand, three hundred and four	1
7	55p or £0.55 Award 2 marks for the correct answer. Award 1 mark for a correct formal method but the incorrect answer. £7.35	2 1
8	3 9 5 Award 1 mark only if all answers are correct.	1
9	20	1
10	(table below) Award 1 mark only if all answers are correct.	1
11	5500	1
12	2383	1
	433	1

Question 10 table:

1000 less	Number	1000 more
1325	2325	3325
7265	8265	9265
3037	4037	5037
4005	5005	6005
0	1000	2000

13

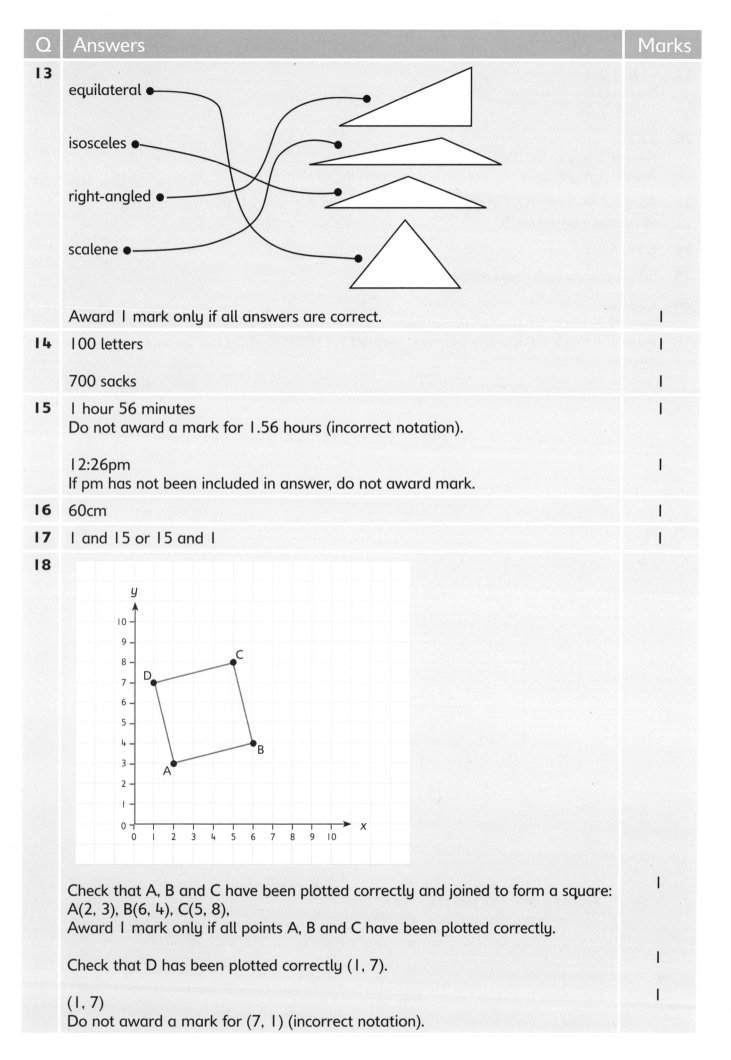

Award 1 mark only if all answers are correct. | 1

14 100 letters | 1

700 sacks | 1

15 1 hour 56 minutes
Do not award a mark for 1.56 hours (incorrect notation). | 1

12:26pm
If pm has not been included in answer, do not award mark. | 1

16 60cm | 1

17 1 and 15 or 15 and 1 | 1

18

Check that A, B and C have been plotted correctly and joined to form a square: | 1
A(2, 3), B(6, 4), C(5, 8),
Award 1 mark only if all points A, B and C have been plotted correctly.

Check that D has been plotted correctly (1, 7). | 1

(1, 7) | 1
Do not award a mark for (7, 1) (incorrect notation).

Q	Answers	Marks
19	4 3 2 5 − 1 8 0 8 2 5 1 7	1
20	£2.50 Award 2 marks for the correct answer. Award 1 mark for a correct formal method for division but an incorrect answer.	2
21	Because the units digit of the answer comes from 7 × 3 = 2<u>1</u>, but the units digit of Ahmet's answer is 5.	1
22	60 children	1
23	30 metres or 3000 centimetres	1
24	£22.25 Award 2 marks for the correct answer. Award 1 mark for a correct formal method for multiplication but an incorrect answer.	2
	Total	**35**

SCHOLASTIC National Curriculum SATs Tests

Q	Answers	Marks
1	Check that all three decimals have been correctly positioned. Ambiguous positioning, or numbers positioned between dashes, should not be awarded a mark. Award 1 mark only if all answers are correct.	1
2	18, 24, 30 Award 1 mark only if all answers are correct.	1
3	2389 + 921 = 1468 ✗ 2389 − 921 = 1468 ✔ 1468 + 921 = 2389 ✔ 1468 − 921 = 2389 ✗	1
4	$\begin{array}{r} 875 \\ \times\ 359 \\ \hline 1234 \end{array}$	1
5	13 chocolates	1
6	4000g	1
	100cm	1
7	0.25 0.5 0.75 Award 1 mark only if all answers are correct.	1
8	£6.80 or 680p Award 2 marks for the correct answer. Award 1 mark for a correct formal method but an incorrect answer.	2
9	3085	1
	4 ones or 4 4 hundreds or 400 4 tens or 40 Award 1 mark only if all answers are correct.	1
	3210	1
10	5 minutes	1
11	$\frac{17}{30}$	1
	$\frac{13}{30}$	1
12	1156 bricks	1

13

five-tenths → 0.5
three-hundredths → 0.03
zero point zero five → 0.05
zero point three → 0.3

Award 1 mark only if all answers are correct.

Marks: 1

14 9p
Award 3 marks for the correct answer.
Award 2 marks for $12 \times 6 = 72$ and $72 \div 8$ = incorrect answer.
Award 1 mark for just $12 \times 6 = 72$.

Marks: 3

15 Check that angles have been named correctly: top left angle is obtuse; top right angle is acute; lower angle is a right angle.
Award 1 mark only if all answers are correct.

Marks: 1

16 96

Marks: 1

17 25

Marks: 1

$\frac{28}{100}$ or $\frac{7}{25}$ or $\frac{14}{50}$
Award 1 mark for $100 - 72 = 28$

Marks: 1

18 £800

Marks: 1

19 3 full cups

Marks: 1

20 212

Marks: 1

28

Marks: 1

21 700cm
If an answer is incorrect, award 1 mark for length of the long side of the shape.
$140 + 35 + 35 = 210$

Marks: 2

22 Check that square has been drawn correctly:
A (3, 8), B (3, 5), C (6, 8), D (6, 5).
Award 1 mark only if all points are plotted correctly.

Marks: 1

23 $\frac{1}{16}$

Marks: 1

Q	Answers	Marks
24	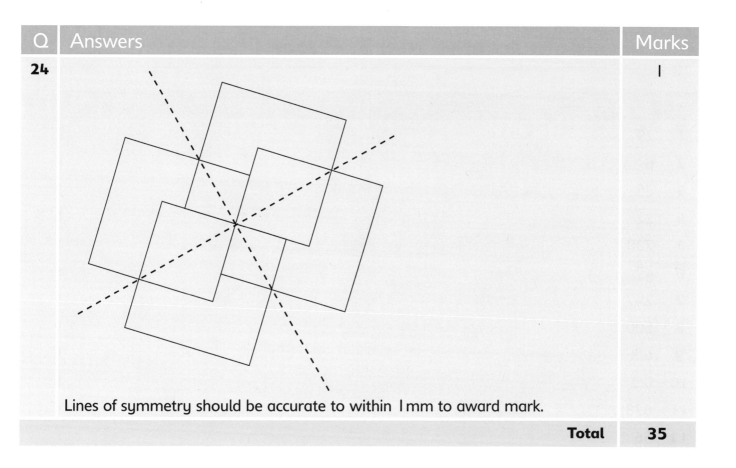	1

Lines of symmetry should be accurate to within 1mm to award mark.

	Total	**35**

Mark scheme Test B: Paper 1 (pages 71–85)

Q	Answers	Marks
1	29	1
2	6	1
3	35	1
4	22	1
5	700	1
6	42	1
7	247	1
8	500	1
9	6.3	1
10	0.3	1
11	678	1
12	36	1
13	4684	1
14	$\frac{3}{5}$	1
15	3562	1
16	$\frac{5}{12}$	1
17	378	1
18	54	1
19	2075	1
20	1601	1
21	4000	1
22	195	1
23	75	1
24	29	1
25	213 Award 1 mark for a correct written method for short division but with one arithmetic error.	2
26	2183	1
27	125	1

SCHOLASTIC National Curriculum SATs Tests

Q	Answers	Marks
28	7862	1
29	165	1
30	$\frac{3}{4}$	1
31	975 Award 1 mark for a correct written method for short multiplication but with one arithmetic error.	2
32	0.25	1
33	1365 Award 1 mark for a correct written method for short multiplication but with one arithmetic error.	2
34	4865	1
35	240	1
36	134 r1 Award 1 mark for a correct written method for short division but with one arithmetic error.	2
	Total	**40**

Q	Answers	Marks
1	○ □ Award 1 mark only if both answers are correct.	1
2	2	1
3	2p	1
	28p	1
	13p	1
4	91, 98, 105 Award 1 mark only if all answers are correct.	1
5	$\frac{1}{2}$, $\frac{1}{3}$, $\frac{1}{6}$ Award 1 mark only if all answers are correct.	1
6	6742	1
7	1 ant 2 pencil 3 dad 4 aeroplane 5 road Award 1 mark only if all answers are correct.	1
	1750mm	1
8	54 blackberries	1
9	555, 999, 1005, 1009, 5999, 9555 Award 1 mark only if all answers are correct.	1
10	7000 2000 6000 Award 1 mark only if all answers are correct.	1
11	4299 children	1

12

Angle	a	b	c	d
Type	Obtuse	Obtuse	Acute	Acute

1

Award 1 mark only if all answers are correct.

An angle that is less than one right angle or less than 90 degrees.   1

| 13 | 115 miles | 1 |

Q	Answers	Marks
14	944 legs Award 2 marks for the correct answer. Award 1 mark for a correct formal written method but an incorrect answer.	2
15	Check that point D has been plotted and labelled correctly. Award mark only if connecting lines are accurate to within 1mm. (7, 7) Check that the centre has been plotted correctly as (5, 5).	1 1 1
16	7 children	1
17	Check that hands have been drawn correctly to show 2:35. 45 minutes or three-quarters of an hour.	1 1
18	£16	1
19	Check that ticks have been written beside these statements: ● All sides are the same length. ● Opposite sides are parallel. ● Opposite angles are equal. Award 1 mark only if all answers are correct.	1
20	$\frac{1}{4}$ 10 apples	1 1
21	$\begin{array}{r} 1\,5\,4\,3 \\ -\ \ 7\,1\,8 \\ \hline 8\,2\,5 \end{array}$ Award 1 mark only for correct answer.	1
22	87 birds Award 2 marks for the correct answer. Award 1 mark for a correct formal method but an incorrect answer.	2
23	£13.50 or 1350p Do not award mark for incorrectly presented price.	1
24	4pm 11pm and 10am	1 1
	Total	**35**

Q	Answers	Marks
1	Check that one triangle and one hexagon have been shaded. Award 1 mark for clear identification of any one of each shape.	1
	triangle (accept equilateral triangle) hexagon Award 1 mark only if both names are correct.	1
2	0.9, 0.91, 0.99, 1.0, 1.1 Award 1 mark only if all answers are correct.	1
3	1 7 8 Award 1 mark only if all answers are correct.	1
4	2p Award 2 marks for the correct answer. Award 1 mark for the correct total of the two books (£14.98) but an incorrect answer.	2
	7 weeks	1
5	60 metres or 60m Award 2 marks for the correct answer. Award 1 mark for the correct perimeter of both squares (40m and 20m) but an incorrect answer.	2
6	−5	1
7	288 miles Award 2 marks for the correct answer. Award 1 mark for a correct formal method but an incorrect answer.	2
8	XXXIV	1
9	1000ml	1
	egg cup mug vase bottle	1
	10 times	1
10	3	1
11	Eight hundred or 800	1
12	2700 seconds Award 2 marks for the correct answer. Award 1 mark for a correct formal method or a correct approach to converting minutes to seconds but an incorrect answer.	2

13

	All sides equal	Opposite sides equal
All angles equal	square	rectangle
Opposite angles equal	rhombus	parallelogram

Award 1 mark only if all answers are correct.

kite   trapezium

Marks: 1, 1

14 1211

7939

Marks: 1, 1

15 0.43

Mark: 1

16

Award 1 mark only if all answers are correct.

Mark: 1

17 $\frac{1}{2}$ of 38

$\frac{5}{8}$

Eye colour	Blue	Not blue
Children	9	15

Award 1 mark only if both answers are correct.

Marks: 1, 1, 1

18 Check that ticks are beside these statements:
Walking is the most popular form of travel.
As many people walk or cycle as use the other types of transport.
Award 1 mark only if both answers are correct.

Mark: 1

19 3565

Mark: 1

Q	Answers	Marks
20	42,871	1
	75,356	1
21	£900 Award 2 marks for the correct answer. Award 1 mark for correctly halving £9000 (answer £4500) but an incorrect answer.	2
	Total	**35**

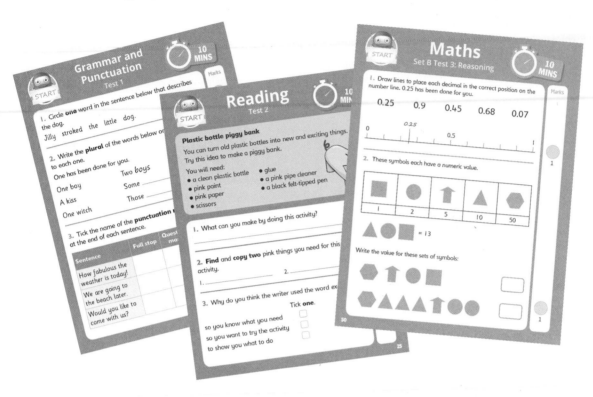